Blowdown

For permissions and information on ordering books, contact
operations@smallharborpublishing.com.

Cover design: Diana Baltag
Interior design: Claire Eder
Editor: Joshua Davis
Publisher: Allison Blevins
Executive Editor: Kristiane Weeks-Rogers
Managing Editor: Bianca Dagostino

BLOWDOWN
JESSICA L. WALSH
ISBN 978-1-957248-64-6
Harbor Editions,
an imprint of Small Harbor Publishing
Special thanks to: The Wild & Precious Life Series and Kristin Vandeventer

Blowdown

Jessica L. Walsh

Harbor Editions
Small Harbor Publishing

Contents

Blowdown

Folly

A wardrobe in an unused room,
or belly of a roll-top desk.

Cedar hope chest in a cellar.
Some neglected garden folly.

I was not ready to be alive,
not the way whole rooms require,

but I spilled onto this land anyway
with all its open snowy fields,

a scared-fierce creature
with neither path nor camouflage.

Five decades in plain sight
and what do I have to show for surviving—

With My Boots On

Whose winged project was I
when I crashed into a pile of dirt
and held it like the front line,
playing king of the hill
the way my mother taught me,
kicking boys in the face
when they came for me,
watching them tumble away.

Bitch, they said, and it's true
I ripped into life
looking for a fight
I can't win
or tap out of.

So give me my accounting.
Pulp this family tree
and make of it a ledger.

Where did that marrow come from.

Whose chicken legs and soft belly.
Who loosed my bones
and clenched my fists.

Who traded beauty for breadth,
gave me guilt without confession.

What gave birth to my debts,
poured the salt of my thirst.

Who made me fall in love
with death and life
in equal parts, robbing graves
to circle skeletons
like a sad birthday party
that ends in sad poetry.

Who holds me here through decades
I believed could never come.

Whose long nights do I keep
when my body tosses to dawn,

who flays and wires my mind
with the same terrible questions,
then binds my head in the silence
of a disappointing séance.

Who are the shadows at my back
from long before my life
that skitter away when I turn my head.

Where are they, the resolute
who wrote my answers.

What part of me was inevitable,
or was I always past the point.

I'm asking: am I my own fault.

The Thing Itself

Every year she assigned me
the work of finding her
in a book of poems,
a few checked with faint pencil.

Secret messages in syllabus,
a relationship palimpsest.

I learned how to find
what's barely there, between
and outside the thing itself.

Thus comes my trade:
fleshing body from femur,
raising house from one truss.

What led me to words?
Wanting.

Museums of History

Our diner's fixture is Jim,
the local history expert,
a man banned from the library
for pressing a knife to the throat
of the girl who worked closing.

He loiters at the counter alone.
Marsha says he's harmless really
but keeps a stool open on either side
and doesn't ask him to move
even when people are waiting—

harmless, yes,
the way men are
when they have all they want
and no one to answer to,

the way my grandfather is
when we pick a good day to visit.

His city's hours from ours,
so big it has a museum about itself
complete with a replica of itself
from a century or so ago,
all cobblestones and hitching posts,
storefronts of corsets, clocks, tonics.
Here it's forever the strolling hours
of quiet evening, dark
but for flickering streetlamps.

Gaslight Village
gives a gutter with no rats,
street free of dirt and dung;

Jim with only a butter knife
piecing out his coconut crème;

my grandfather quiet,
walking away.

What the Lake Gives Back

Choked fish silver the surface
as drought pulls back the curtain
on all we hid there:
beer cans and liquor bottles,
TVs and fridges.
A washing machine.

Heat cracks wide the mud
to hand back our bones,
sometimes whole skeletons,
mostly the odd tibia or vertebrae.

One skull near another.
If they sank together
or if one sent the other
they won't tell.

Our people die with their secrets
sealed in their mouths.

Look. We drank too much.
Couldn't be bothered
with permits and long rides
out to the county dump.
We had stuff but not money.
We settled our business.

I'm sorry to our sewn-shut past
when I write what we tried to hide,
layering fresh flesh onto fossils
like life itself is nothing
but imagination.

Posterity, 1974–92

She records what she wants
to be true: we came happily

and enjoyed our visits, praying thanks
for pot roasts and scalloped potatoes

at a properly set table.
We slept well and awoke in good spirits.

We never wanted to leave.
She loved us.

Who lied and how,
who performed or edited,

I can't say anymore.
I know I gagged on all of it,

salted gristle and grace.
At her table I learned obligation,

and I bristle at it still. After every visit,
my mother lit a cigarette in the car.

The Women's Years, 1943–5

During the war, she dotes on a baby
who will become my gentle father,
gives him cream cheese cake
and dime-store toys.

He learns a toddler's Polish
from his babcia next door,
words for bottom and milk and darling.

She prays the war will never end,
that her husband will leave them be.

Or she prays the opposite:
that he'll be home tomorrow.

Reader. I don't know
whether she prays at all.

I can't find her in my imagining—
I've written her to shreds,
but she sheds lines
and slides away.

What I know: my grandfather
comes home from war
and keeps fighting,
his house a combat zone
where no one is safe.

Multiples of One

Take the one who ditched Michigan for Hawaii,
waited till her six kids were full-grown
before she left the drunk who'd hurt them all.

What I keep is one visit: we ate fish
and looked out her window to green mountains.
I remember a waterfall, and I think that's wrong—

I added it, most likely, from a picture of Oahu,
trying to stretch flash into novel,
like I could write family into my life.

I can never come back, she told my dad
when he sent her a ticket, then kept repeating herself
until he stopped trying at all.

My beautiful cousin tells me over sweet coffee
that she owes her whole life
to the same woman who missed mine.

This is a warning against story,
against exactly what you are trying to do.
There's no hope these ghosts will settle

when they can't even choose a form,
forever flipping tête-bêche.
A grandmother who loved one

and let the other fall away.
A mom who hugged her kids
but fed the wolf who hunted them.

The Needle Meets the Vinyl

Someone's getting hurt tonight,
you know from the music who
and whether to dodge or watch—
how rough the relief of your reprieve
how sick the ease of another's bruise.

Poets declare *you* is how the *I* hides
and you can't say different,
you learned early to hide,
that *I am here* means *here I am.*
Switch the record, come get me.

You split into a stable of yous:
good girl quiet girl skinny girl
busy girl working girl gone girl,
you are all of them just in case
one of you is not in trouble.

Plymouth, 1620

Rank and faith both fake,
he was merely their mercenary,
and once the pilgrims settled,
once he'd bordered the colony
with bones and bodies,
he wandered away for wealth,
had kids who had kids
and so on.

And here I am.

I'm invited to join a *society*
where stories go for glory,
the soft side of history, cushioned,
the past through frosted glass—

like when I find the ancestor
whose farm was a stop
on the Underground Railroad,

and God I want to put a period there,
pause for applause.
Look, I want to say,
I'm one of the good ones.

But his land was damp
with the blood of Seneca and Erie
who fought to stay.

What I'm saying is
there are ways for me to feel good
or ways to see the truth,
not both.

I could be somebody's good guy
before I die.
I'm definitely a bad one
in ways I don't yet know.

I dug up this chalky dirt

and now it's mine to carry.

Nothing shakes my dreams
free of bones.

Unfit, 1929

Not youngest but smallest
none weaker than him
blue eyes crescented purple
skin sheer over bones
like he'd never seen the sun

Does he ever see the sun
the Hygiene Men ask
and they take him
from his mother
who knows the fact of runts
and makes small fuss

The rest eat more at supper
and their quiet stomachs
fill the space for missing him

Family Day at the Preventorium, 1930

Easter at the warehouse of weak boys
means a chance of family.

Faces crowd at open windows,
pink with newfound health

or desperation. They call to parents
who can't hear them but yell back anyway.

Knowing is impossible from afar.
Distance is the singular safety.

After waving and failed words,
fathers nod and families turn to leave

until another holiday, another year,
whenever the Hygiene Men decide

that a boy is fit. Or hopeless. Done.
Only then can he cross the lawn.

   ***

One day a boy goes home, but *different*,
his sister will say. *I couldn't even hug him.*

The new pink in his pale cheeks
is not evidence of thriving

but the flag signaling rage,
warning of singular danger.

He is wild, impossible.
He is unleashed.

   ***

Even before I could write his name
I learned the flush of a coming strike.

Because of him, I know at least two ways
to leave every room I enter,

and I carry at least two ways
to take a man down.

He was hurt as a boy.
I want the truth to mean more than it does.

God forgive me:
I forgive him nothing.

Mausoleum

I tried to rope myself
to people of the living world,
to anchor love,
as tied to this side as I am to the other,

but I'm still the child
who ran half a block to the cemetery
and waited for anyone to come.

I wanted so long
that I fell in with the dead,
their constancy and softness
my secret bowered nook
even when I turned away from them,
and again, back
to this ridiculous loneliness.

I clutch the veil
like a clump of hair circling the drain,
which happens more now, stress or age.
I get close but not beyond,
tangled up and hanging on.
I wear it like a shawl
holding back night's chill
when I walk home alone.

I Keep Trying to Tell You

How my skin tightened and pinched
like scales were pushing through to shield me.

How I could not swear if he was one man
or many, peeling into flickering replicas
until he covered every door and corner.

How his laugh cut and slashed across the room
like flames chasing gin.

How I still can't find a word for what he was, just that
whenever he came around, something came with him.

The Silence

a cento from the journals of Marjorie Del Weldin Lane (1910–2006)

I finally took out the obituaries.
I hadn't wanted to read them.
I do not understand my feeling in this.
Now the papers are yellowed
with the years.

The sun came out this early evening
and I thought of the silent space
of fields and meadow
all around their home.
A rough recollection,
a turbulent year—
bleak—lonely—humiliating.

The cruel cut—
the awful silent finality—
the terrible grandeur and power of it—
those who were here and now are gone.

Shadows of lives before
all around us,
a still quiet awareness
of time passing.
Time eternally putting things,
even present things, in the past—
the sun—the leaves moving.
Time all around us—
so silent but rushing! rushing!

I May Never See You Again

Every day he was about to die
though no one told him

In those times
sickness grew from its name

Today may be his last
and *today* again

He barely spoke
and slept fitfully

Today he seems well
but is he really

His daughters walk on straw
say *I love you* over and over

They graduate early
and marry quickly

have their own daughters
because this might be it

They rush life under threat
Don't you want him to see

Thirty years pass
before he dies

Every prophecy of death
is someday true

***

The Hemlock Society guide to suicide
tucked between classics

They found it when she died
at 96 of old age

She didn't use the hatch
but whether she ever tried

can be added to the catalog
of all she vaulted away

***

I don't know if life or line
makes me keep trying

to try to kill myself
What keeps me alive

Remember how I starved myself bloodless
I could hear my brittle ribs clatter

until I fell in love and licked
peanut butter off of his spoon

Later on drove drunk enough
that I couldn't read my speed

aimed at the train trestle west of Hy-Vee
but a girl crossed the road

She wasn't me so probably deserved
to live or maybe to die

I don't know what punishment is now—
if penance is another day or its absence

Even now I have 89 ambien
in a bottle behind my socks

Look I know I'm going to lose this life
but I want to call it

the way my mom quit her job too early
because leaving on her own terms

was better than severance

We were stubborn broke

These days she cries in the car
outside the food pantry

calls me and says she wants to die
Calls me again the next day

***

Some people
my people

cuff themselves to death
and keep walking

Punchline, 1981

He was a fun drunk
says Vern from the VFW
after he dies in a rage
swinging at the nurse

and I say yes.
Hysterical.

His slot machine, rebuilt
to roll out a can of beer
when you pulled the arm,
a jackpot of room-temperature Schiltz
he'd offer to my folks on ice
as he told us about Tijuana or Windsor
like he'd traveled all the world.

He promised me and my sister
that if we were good girls, he'd leave us
the Pabst clock he won off old man Meijer

and maybe even the rain lamp
with the naked lady in the middle
that I couldn't stop staring at.

My parents left us there once,
risking the hours to shop for Christmas—

we were Santa-aged still
and they had no one else—

and came back to find us hiding,
sobbing, clutched together in a corner.

On the ride home, my father cried.
He never took us there again.
We didn't get the clock or the lamp.

Could be Vern took them,
to remember the good times.

Vacant Lot, 1984

Stay close enough for Kool-Aid
or Band-Aids handed out at the screen door

but away in a way
that gives mom space
for a cigarette
and Sanka in the kitchen.

Head for the lot,
thick with weeds and trees,
tall oaks that have never been owned,
ground rolling with acorns
ready for a boy's slingshot.

Remember you're away in a way
that consents to boys being boys.

Hang by your knees
upside-down on rough branches
swing until your face purples,

but the price is a shirt pulled up or down,
a leg rubbed for stubble.

Learn to be mad
but not to fight,
learn to live mad and quiet.

Run home when the streetlights come on,
not before, staying silent
in the long shadow of a woman
who has hung on through worse.

In a Meadow of Warheads

1.

I clean a clean house, fold
fitted sheets and underwear,
wash down garbage cans–

but who am I to fool grief?

I don't deserve to be spared.
Scraped bare, my bones buzz,
eyes tunnel to black panic.

I crack, I fail, I breech
like a levee hit with dynamite.

When I swallow half
of that bourbon marked for guests
I hate my own joy,

the way I felt in labor
when the epidural hit:

an ecstasy of failure.

2.

My genes call next in Russian roulette.
I'm from time bombs, minus time,
born in a meadow of warheads.

Part of me stays monstrous.

Picture me as creature on the slab,
Dr. Frankenstein above me,
keening for lightning to flip my switch.
His folly is seeing me blank-slate.

There are lives gone bad before starting,
I'm saying, ways to stop the bottle

before it ever hits my lips.

I don't know which part was failure,
awakening or the moment before.

I'm only safe without my life.

3.

I brought no one along
from my squalor years.
Most are dead, all gone.

Here is the only proof
at least part of me
wants to survive.

Self-Portrait in Bile and Glass, 1999

Even now I am the woman
who woke up beside an off-limits man
and ran to his doorless bathroom,
threw up into the mirror,
met my own watery eyes
through that first clear wave
of plastic bottle vodka,
watched it slide down my chin
and the reflection of my chin,
down this body I threw away
on any man who got hard for me—
the woman who collected lust like money
and I don't know if I drank
to stand fucking them or drank
to see myself worth fucking
but nothing worked,
nothing changed me.
Even now I see myself through
rivulets of vodka and spit.
No picture is more honest.

Stop One Clock, 1992

Remind me how she stole
all the pills in the house
the day I graduated

and I will answer
that I am glad she came,

ate piece after piece of cake with me,
laughed loud at my father's jokes,

that in her smoke-low voice,
her quick joy,
I heard her
as she should have been.

I can't be convinced
I didn't love her.

The Coldwater State School, 1927

Weeks after she buries her family,
she stands on a wrap-around porch

where rocking chairs tilt empty
in bitter winter wind.

On the threshold
of a time she'll never name,
the years that chase her
like a wolf fattening on shame.

She lives on the run
from what stays leashed
tight to her heels,

learns what it means
to be pursued. Watched.

How punishment follows pause.

Proper posture
for perpetual vigilance.

Which hand
holds the knife.

Where the knife belongs
when it's a message.

What the message is
that can slow the wolf
long enough

for her to try polite society,
where people have people.
She bakes a cake, chiffon,
serves on crystal plates
with punch from a crystal bowl.

But true ladies
know lard from butter.

She learns then that
it was all for nothing.
Quiet constant panic.
Striving. Disguising.

Nothing covers
the marks of the wolf.

Headwaters

He never apologized.
Still, she keeps his coffee full,
draws smiley faces on the bill.

Relentless kindness
he can hardly handle
years after he gossiped her out of school
because he couldn't say
he was jealous.

When her son goes wrong
and deputies sidle,
the man lies easily. They all do.
Nope, haven't seen him.

Some secrets are debts settled.
What's unsaid turns apology.

Let empty spaces
tally up amends.

Iowa, 2000

Goal: deep cover.
I work speech, teeth, obliques

but I get made every time.

In the end it's fork and knife,
or fork sideways to play knife.

Or the drink I order
when I'm already drunk,
when I've *gulped*
because gulp is to sip
as eat is to nibble.
Appetite's an airhorn
announcing an imposter.

Tuxedoed waiters
circle galleries with silver trays,
arch their eyebrows when I take two,
nod to square men at doors
who check guest lists,
watch me like a shoplifter.

It could be my own party,
the dinner I split on three cards.

I open my mouth,
that's what it comes down to—

and they know.

A Girl Walks Out of a Bar

When I asked my professor for a letter,
he said *What you should do is open a bar.*
Jackson or Flint, maybe. Someplace rough.

He saw me. Knew that I'd never stop
being the kind of woman
you can still call a *broad*,
that I would always be one minute
from starting shit
I lacked the sense to regret.
He knew my vowels would stay high in my nose,
that I'd wrinkle up like a smoker no matter what.

But he didn't get that I'd already learned
how to be five animals at once.
How to survive in hostile places
like our old money campus,
like the low chair beside his desk.

He shot himself
before he could see me living
off the long con of a job just like his.

I'm not above believing I won.

I Cry All Morning and Pick a Fight in the Afternoon

I hate myself for both
but I also get to hate
Tim the librarian.
Breaks up the circle.

If I'm honest, I'm trying to stay angry.
Builds muscle.
Get mad, my mother used to say
when my crying
used up her patience.
Anger gets shit done.

All alternatives are flimsy,
fragile like the ice
that broke under a wolf up north—
when she clawed her way out,
onlookers cheered,
but I know better.
A wet wolf in snowy woods
most likely froze alone.

Bitter beats crying
over life on a planet
that can't wait to kill you.

A tug captain I know has a tattoo
that says *BITCH* in a big red heart.
For the lakes, he tells me.
Mother Nature. What a fuckin' bitch.
He knows the score:
life's enemy territory.

But lately my anger can't hold.
Tim the librarian
wears off fast.
Everyone's down too far to kick.
Around me, all implosions,
the whole earth
a white flag waving.

I think I'm all I have
left to fight with. *BITCH*
in my own red heart.

My doctor gives me pills,
says take one only when it's really bad.

These days it's always terrible,
and it could always be worse.

I know all the ways how.

She tells me I won't feel like this forever.

She can only mean that one cold thing.

Thine Is the Kingdom

I'm quick with bread
but near impossible with trespasses.
I forget forgiveness every time, always have,
even when my grandmother promised a quarter
for a proper recitation.

I knew her disappointment
before I knew what to call it.
She died still hoping I'd grow out of myself.

But even now I leave out the part about apologies,
skip right to a dinner roll stuffed with margarine,
and another one the next time the basket passes.

Forgive me that, I guess.
Forgive me anything.

Pretty Life

Every woman I talk to
wants a way out of her pretty life,
though lately I don't talk to many people,
mostly my dad who is dead
and the picture of a friend
who went the painkiller route
and off all grids,
moved to a farm of all things,
and I say to her picture,
what the fuck, girlie,
are you doing there,
how did it happen—

Every woman wants—
I want to say—
this is a good life, I love my people
and I'm dying to get out of here,
no one's princess in a tower,
a hag in a mop closet,
Bitch Radley,
asking myself
what the fuck, girlie,
are you doing here,
how did this happen.

What She Fell For, 1905

The man erased
but for his lies—

A city fresh from itself,
phoenixed into bricks

Night song, day song,
third rail buzz

Stores ten stories
to stained glass sky

Wind off waves
into sun-gold rooms

Feather bed
without chickens

Girl to clean
and girl to cook

Piano for no one
but her, brand new

Away, away,
to future perfect

Bronson, 1985

A dozen crows face north,
their heads black compass needles.

Beyond them, green-grey clouds spill closer.

Rain spits thick,
winds move towards roar,

and still the crows don't move.

My grandmother pulls me from the porch,
rushes us to the spider-filled cellar I hate.
We wait.

Later the yard is rumpled
but empty.

I'm sure all the crows died
and I'm just as sure
they fled to safety.

There's a Cemetery with No Stones

My uncle, I hear,
was gentle and kind,

a florist with a warm laugh
and a house above Golden Gate.

It's certified that he was born
but I can't find how he died.

I'm transferred to an old man,
a volunteer retired from his city job.

His voice is weary grief:
How did he die? Alone,

in a wing sealed to visitors.
There wasn't even a word yet.

       *   *   *

One day a friend disappears,
removes her certified life

from search and source.
I find no news of death.

Neither can I prove
she lives, or ever lived.

The back of a photo reads *Martha*
in my own handwriting.

I ask my other friends,
Was she real? Do you remember?

and we doubt ourselves more
as years slough away

until light shines through memory
and still the ache endures.

*   *   *

I live in words of loss.
I'm not ready to let go of people I can't prove.

I know a cemetery with no stones,
full of wanting.

Dangers of the Flesh

Let it be said that I ignored warnings,
ran shore to blanket
my hands full of dead alewives,
my palms silvered still
when I dropped them in the sand
at my cursing mother's feet.

I took to vultures and roadkill,
drawn to piles of what was alive,
fur and flies and stink.

My mother would snap *Leave it!*
the way I yell at my dog
when he lunges for goose shit
or the trash can full of tampons.

The only trophies I could keep:
bones picked clean to white,
stripped of danger.

These days I write my own skeleton
but for every summer of crows,
there's a long winter under snow.

I leave myself exposed
and still the flesh clings.

The Dying Year, 1926

Like scared horses
they race wild to get away:
mother
father
grandmother
grandfather.

A girl not grown
but grown enough
to raise her brother
sets off to survive,
works farms or schoolhouses,
stays within a day
of four sunburned graves
she never visits.

Whether she resents her brother
who wants more and more
or rages at her dead for running
she never tells.

Decades line up
to carry her forward
into a long long life
of hard work
and light sleep,
of keeping her brother close
and her mouth closed
in a cold tight line.

After the Audit, Coldwater State Home, 1928

Nurses gossip huddled in halls,
scared the worst is coming:
reform means an end
to what they've learned to do and done,
their bread and butter gone,
children's bread suddenly buttered
in a hall heated with coal
that staff can't steal anymore.

In the system one side survives:
mercenary nurses called *angel-makers*
who cozy up with undertakers
for a cut per coffin,

or the children dropped here,
orphans at best,
most hopeless already,
convicted by birth.

Old nurses resign,
younger ones come,
schooled to keep every child
just this side of alive—

like the girl who turns seventeen,
becomes staff by day
but stays ward by night.

She stands on a line
and there, she hesitates.

The Boy in the Barn, 1929

His overalls are fire-ribboned
gas-fueled and then gone.

She swats out flames bare-handed
and their skin marries in blisters.

Threads of her palms settle
in the gelled red craters of his body.

She carries him to the doctor's house
then returns to her room behind the school.

The next day she wears church gloves
to chalk perfect letters on the boards.

When students, squirrely with gossip,
ask her what happened, she is hard silence.

The boy dies twelve days later.
The story is already gone.

Florida, 1983

My father warns us of alligators,
but danger seems impossible
below the mirrored moss.

It's not the bite, he says,
holding my hand, walking me away,
but how the gator holds you under,
never lets you back to the surface.

Four decades later,
my dad breathes his last
like he can't reach the air,
his lungs pooled and clogged.

I try to write about him,
the miracle of his goodness,
how his eyes were never bluer
than the moment he stopped blinking.
I want every line to be beautiful.
Every line could pull me under.

I Fed No Birds

Once in the woods
I was alone—

only once was I alone—

only once
I was in the woods
was I alone—

and there in the woods
I spilled
cold-hearted
and careless—

not once did I think
of the living
who'd yelled after me
that they couldn't
do anything alone—

once I was monstrous
whether here or there—

if the woods
were the worst of me
it was only once—

Rescue

My mother takes in shelter dogs.
It's not principle but budget,
she's too poor to have stances.

She calls them the clearance rack—
three-legged black dog,
jealous, neurotic terrier,
adults already, messed up
from whatever came before.

That's where she lingers: before.

She guesses what happened
to make this dog scared of singing
or that dog lunge at children

and she believes herself,
telling us about the owner who sang
while he kicked and burned

or how the unmothered children
took turns on torture.

What they come with, they keep.
She doesn't train her dogs
but instead bans music in the house,
yells at kids to get back.

It's not the dogs' fault, she frowns.
She gives leeway to a bad past,
real or imagined, like blame
is the same as forgiveness.

Stern of Will

If genes print
what makes a bitch,
I had no chance.
That switch was flipped
before my lungs sucked air
and stuck on screech for weeks.
Mom smoked Trues
and rocked me, pacing out fury.

Still my anger burns, fed by itself,
a gift of every generation,
a curse of cursing,
one to the next.

I don't blame our first stern mother
for giving me enough to thrive.
I own my temper, my hot decisions,
the way I force my will on love
to craft the list of who I'll keep
and who I'll toss to wolves or men.

The records echo over and over:
these bitches run their lives like war,
positive of mind and force.

Heraldry

I can't count on kindness
when I call to my dead,
nor that they're proud of me,
fussing soft-handed with words
while strangers shovel the drive.

Blend all our crests and legends.
Bannered above my name,
not Latin but the clipped English
of a woman tying her apron:
There's work to be done.

Ditch Digger, 1848

The ship spills hundreds of hungry men,
a wave of bones crashing onto docks.

Company men promise meals, money, mass.
The skeletal head west, desperate,

part of what will be called a horde
when their labor is used up.

Ditch becomes canal,
links river to lakes to the same ocean

they crossed, to rough beaches
where waves lap against their absence.

Tonight I listen to Lake Michigan,
its whitecaps churning sand and stone,

a gruff percussive roar, a song
of the waters' give and take.

Life Piled on Life, 1865

After battle, he goes home but doesn't stay,
maybe tired of farm life and his actual wife
who is different than she'd been at a distance.

Could be it's too easy, home and family,
that he misses the indifference of war,
the confusion of blues and greys in mud,
men falling noble or clumsy towards death
while he keeps himself just this side of it,

and so he leaves again to Lake Michigan
where he rides the rise and fall of danger,
surviving through a dozen Novembers
until old age drops him at the city docks.

I'd like to think he rests then, content
with Indiana and his vault of tales.

More likely he walks away from the lake
the way I do every time I make shore,
wondering if I've been blessed to reach land
or spit out from the grey-blue mouth of home.

Forge

When it's time to empty
my dad's back shed,
I prop the door
with the first thing I find,
an antler, its janky angles
stronger than they should be,
from an animal felled a century ago
by a giant man called The Major
who cast the pellets himself at his forge—
a Paul Bunyan of war and corn
who came home from Atlanta on foot
with three rebel swords and no story,
just the answer, "It was a fair fight,"
which is all I say when they ask me
about the scars I carry,
where my skin came back
thicker, piled upon itself
in tough, ropey lines,
I did you proud, Major.
It was a fair fight.

Emptied Out

The string of things I haven't done could reach
from here to every place I've never been:
New York, Golden Corral, an orgy, Rome.

They say that's a bucket list. My great-grandfather
worked his neighbors' farms to keep his own,
carrying the tin lunch pail that's now on my shelf.

Some days he probably swung it empty from dark to dark
hoping someone could toss in day-old bread or a nickel.
My guess is he'd be awed by all we have. Or mad at what he didn't.

My dad griped that we barely had a pot to piss in, but *barely*
does a lot there. We had a pot to piss in, I'm saying, even Pizza Hut
on paydays, a quarter for Pac-Man if we were good and lucky.

Ain't no hole in the washtub, sang my mom,
and she was right, though there was a hole in the back room ceiling
that filled the chili pot when it rained hard and long.

So I've never been to Brazil, but I've never gone hungry,
always had bread, bologna, a coffee can full of grease
way at the back of the fridge, second shelf.

I think I'd like to finish my life with whatever it takes to endure it.
Beyond that, I don't know. The smell of his pillow. A dog.
Maybe a vodka to close it out. Enough.

My Disheveling

To my body:
brick house
turned tear-down.

To the way men skip me,
the safety of my face unmade,
the cozy Carhartt lump of me
alone.

To time unbothered
at coffee shop
and hardware store.

To the scowl of my ancestors,
women who pushed a plow
and killed their dinner.

For them I take up space.

For them I keep
the chaff on my wheat.

I unleash myself,
disheveling toward the day
when men give up their bus seats,
not chivalrous but uneasy
at the sight of a woman eroding.

I am ready to join
my ghosts and crones.

Big Hands

I talk with my hands,
talk big for a creature
with a skittering heart.

My hands span 10 keys easy,
could palm a basketball
which I never tried
because it was surrender
to do things big girls do.

Every breath is a jump scare
in a barfight body—
do you believe that?
Do you know what it's like
to be a ballbuster, terrified?

Scary is a beard for scared,
ask any Goth girl. Not me,
not in my body when bony
was part of the Goth deal.
Even after the hungry year
I had the wrong bones,
big bones.

I am big-boned, as it were.
My bones are a heavy bag to carry
in my big hands

and it's nice not to break when I fall
because me and gravity
are on-again off-again
even with huge feet—

she has huge feet, my boyfriend said,
huge, and I was mad
the way I'm mad when I get a ticket
for running a light–
mad because it's true.

Still I'd like to try being breakable.
It's what the men love,
men with wild hair
and sinewy philosophies,
the men who own presses
and trust funds
and guns
but will only admit the first.

I'd like to give the word *tiny* a spin,
see if my revolution
gets an adorable shoe in the door
and gives me a chance to rest.
I am so tired of kicking it down.

Distraction

God, Carson says, was just
about to create justice

but made instead a dragonfly,
placing pretty over right.

Must have seemed fair to Keats
with his bit on truth and beauty—

though left to judge each other,
humans made ugly a crime.

And beauty has a hell of a job—
I get why she passed me by.

She was bound to skip a baby here and there
like Santa missing chimneys.

Poor kids who got no Christmas gifts
went to church for answers

the way I'm steered to YouTube
where I am taught to trompe my own l'oeil.

Back at the sink, washed clean,
my face is my regrettable face.

No beauty, no justice, not even the shimmer
that tosses dragonfly clear of common,

just composite of what my bloodline gave me
and the hoofmarks of what I've put it through.

Truth, though, in droves—
just last week I got in trouble at work
for looking like I felt:
so very sick of their shit.

It's not a horrible thing to know
that the truth of my face is not beauty,

to shear one point off the triangle,
collapse the syllogism.

God meant to make me beautiful
and instead created a dragonfly.

11:11

I'm stuck again
between the past
and a blank page.

But this poem is different:
you're home while I write,
and you change everything.

If I can speak truth
into reality
that's what I want
for you:

Change everything.

Elegy, As Allowed

In the minutes before the day began
I read that a good man died,
a man I knew from before,
and I placed grief neatly on the list
of needs that needed me. He'd get it.
He knew work and its many forms,
how it spared no one, least of all
folks like us who came from folks like ours.
He knew me and my many forms,
that I would hold on through the day
until night came quiet and solitary,
that I'd fill dark hours with his death,
wake up with swollen eyes, and work.

Teeth

I fell hard & then harder,
maybe tripped
in childhood's wild.
That's the story I have
and I look for no other.

When I woke up I had a stuffed Grover
and four pouring holes.
My gums couldn't stop my tongue,
my tongue couldn't stop slipping lipward.
I said *thit* for *sit*, *Jethica* of myself,
and nothing when the kids laughed.

I spoke only back-mouthed words
until my mom went back to work,
put money down for a retainer
from the dentist whose kids I played with,
who probably gave us a discount
no one would ever speak of.

At the brickwork college on a green hill
where prep school kids laugh at my town
everyone has good teeth

except cafeteria workers and slow-moving women
who clean dorm halls and common rooms.
I try for their eyes. I want to smoke
with them behind buildings,
complain about the rich kids.

But to the cleaning women I'm a rich kid.
To rich kids I'm a redneck turned ringer,
a rural girl with ACTs to boost the mean.

My teeth are good, my grades better,
and the people I can talk to won't talk to me.
I have no lisp, nor language to use.

Pyre

A minute is the last time that minute will ever happen

No wonder it's exhausting just existing
having to love nonstop because this love right now
is over before you can say it but I'm not done with love

Someone told me I write too much about fire
and I felt like he'd tried to slash my wrists

Don't blame the fire it's just trying to survive
jumping and creeping to the next new loss
like it will never run out of fuel like it doesn't need fuel

One day it will be the last fire of this season
and one day it will be the last fire
and I'll be telling you I love you through the thin white smoke

Bone Road

I think I want to let you go

I wanted you to tell me
why it hurts so much to be alive
and what part you had in me

what you started and ended

how you lasted through catastrophe
or made amends for causing it

I wanted you to be why
I'm what I am

to tell me how
I can leave myself behind

But you're drops of water
in the river
not the river
I was dipped in
when I first took breath
Lethe's opposite
anointing me
with perpetual remembering

I asked too much of you

Let me ask too much of myself
for whatever's left of this raggedy life

I release you to the road
where I'll find you again

Acknowledgments

"The Needle Meets the Vinyl" and "Posterity," *Painted Bride Quarterly*

"I Keep Trying to Tell You," *Spoon River Poetry Review*

"What the Lake Gives Back" (as "Inheritance") and "Pretty Life," *Lily Poetry Review*

"Dangers of the Flesh." *MER*

"Big Hands," *West Trestle*

"Ditch Digger, 1848," *Great Lakes: An Anthology*

"Folly," *River Dog.*

"Family Day, 1930," "Forge," and "Multiples of One" (as "Note to Self") *Bloodlore.* Anthology by *White Stag*

"Bronson, 1985," *Museum of Americana*

"Emptied Out," *SWWIM.* Republished in *Painted Bride Quarterly.*

"The Boy in the Barn" and "Girl Walks Out of a Bar," *Gamut*

"Thine is the Kingdom" and "Pyre." *White Stag*

"Push" *Pirene's Fountain*

"Vacant Lot, 1984," "Stop One Clock," and "Headwaters," *Public School Poetry*

"11:11" (as "For Stella") *The Going Away Country*

Notes

"The Silence" is taken from various journals of my grandmother, Marjorie Del Weldin Lane. In writing this piece, I did not alter the order of any words, though I did draw from various portions of her journals in a non-chronological fashion.

"Life Piled on Life" is a line in *Ulysses* by Alfred Tennyson, "...Life piled on life / Were all too little, and of one to me."

"11:11" is for my daughter, Stella.

Thanks

I owe my gratitude to so many who helped me in the creation of *Blowdown*.

Thank you to everyone at Small Harbor for taking on *Blowdown*, especially editors Allison Blevins and Kristiane Weeks-Rogers as well as Dustin Brookshire, who put it in front of them. Josh Davis was a keen and generous editor.

For research, my thanks to: James Edstrom, librarian and historian; the Branch County (Michigan) Public Library; the government offices of Marin County, California; the Archives of Western Michigan University; and the National Archives. Each helped fill in some of the innumerable blanks in our family's history.

Harper College granted me sabbatical in fall 2024, allowing me to write full time for four months. Time is a form of privilege.

Jennifer Franklin worked with me to order and revise the manuscript; her insight and guidance cannot be overstated. Early readers who encouraged me included Elizabeth Strauss Friedman, Amy Milligan, and Cypress Milligan.

My husband, Robert, reminds me to always play my own game. Our daughter, Stella, carries all the best of those who came before us, a brilliant reminder of the promise of the future.

Blowdown is in memory of my ancestors. May my life testify to the good among you, and make amends for the bad.

Jessica L. Walsh is the author of three previous collections: *Book of Gods and Grudges, The List of Last Tries and How to Break My Neck*. Her work has appeared on the *Best American Poetry Blog* and journals like *RHINO, Painted Bride Quarterly, Whale Road Review, Crab Creek Review*, and many more. Originally from Ludington, Michigan, she currently lives outside of Chicago and teaches at a community college. For more information, see jessicalwalsh.com.

About Small Harbor Publishing

Small Harbor Publishing is a 501c3 nonprofit organization. Our goal is to publish unique and diverse voices. We are a feminist press, and we are committed to diversity and inclusion. We strive to bring new voices to a devoted and expanding readership.

Small Harbor Publishing began in 2018 with the first issue of *Harbor Review*. The magazine is an online space where poetry and art converse. *Harbor Review* quickly grew and now publishes reviews and runs multiple micro chapbook competitions, including the Washburn Prize and the Editor's Prize.

In July 2020, Small Harbor Publishing was officially incorporated and began Harbor Editions. Harbor Editions accepts submissions through a chapbook open reading period, a hybrid chapbook open reading period, the Marginalia Series, and the Laureate Prize.

In 2023, Harbor Anthologies began with a mission to promote texts that explore social justice issues and highlight marginalized writers.

If you would like to support Small Harbor Publishing, visit our "About" page at: smallharborpublishing.com/about.

www.ingramcontent.com/pod-product-compliance
Lightning Source LLC
Chambersburg PA
CBHW020214090426
42734CB00008B/1072